discover more
Exploring Primary Sources

Exploring Washington's Farewell Address

Sarah Schmidtt

IN ASSOCIATION WITH

Published in 2025 by Britannica Educational Publishing (a trademark of Encyclopædia Britannica, Inc.)
in association with The Rosen Publishing Group, Inc.
2544 Clinton Street, Buffalo, NY 14224

Copyright © 2025 by Encyclopædia Britannica, Inc. Britannica, Encyclopædia Britannica, and the Thistle logo are registered trademarks Encyclopædia Britannica, Inc. All rights reserved.

Rosen Publishing materials copyright © 2025 The Rosen Publishing Group, Inc. All rights reserved.

Distributed exclusively by Rosen Publishing.
To see additional Britannica Educational Publishing titles, go to rosenpublishing.com.

All rights reserved. No part of this book may be reproduced in any form without permission in writing from the publisher, except by a reviewer.

Editor: Brianna Propis
Cover Design: Michael Flynn
Interior Design: Rachel Rising

Photo Credits: Cover (series background) Dai Yim/Shutterstock.com; Cover ronstik/Shutterstock.com; p. 4 Washington, George. George Washington Papers, Series 1, Exercise Books, Diaries, and Surveys -99, Subseries 1A, Exercise Books -1747: Forms of Writing, and The Rules of Civility and Decent Behavior in Company and Conversation, ante 1747. Ante, 1747. Manuscript/Mixed Material. Retrieved from the Library of Congress, <www.loc.gov/item/mgw1a.001/>.; p. 5 https://en.wikipedia.org/wiki/File:Gilbert_Stuart_Williamstown_Portrait_of_George_Washington.jpg; p. 6 https://en.wikipedia.org/wiki/File:General_George_Washington_at_Trenton_by_John_Trumbull.jpeg; p. 7 https://en.m.wikipedia.org/wiki/File:Official_Presidential_portrait_of_Thomas_Jefferson_(by_Rembrandt_Peale,_1800).jpg; p. 9 https://en.m.wikipedia.org/wiki/File:Scene_at_the_Signing_of_the_Constitution_of_the_United_States.jpg; p. 9 ungvar/Shutterstock.com; p. 10 https://en.m.wikipedia.org/wiki/File:Washington%27s_Inauguration.jpg; p. 11 DT phots1/Shutterstock.com; p. 12 https://en.m.wikipedia.org/wiki/File:Reproduction-of-the-1805-Rembrandt-Peale-painting-of-Thomas-Jefferson-New-York-Historical-Society_1.jpg; p. 13 Jacinto Escaray/Shutterstock.com; p. 14 CK Foto/Shutterstock.com; p. 15 National Heritage Museum, Lexington, MA; p. 16 Manuscripts and Archives Division, The New York Public Library. "Farewell address" The New York Public Library Digital Collections. 1796. https://digitalcollections.nypl.org/items/5eaa18b6-d3b5-7de3-e040-e00a18066263; p. 17 The Gilder Lehrman Collection, on deposit at The Pierpont Morgan Library, GLC 185; kilic inan/Shutterstock.com; p. 18 Halytskyi Olexandr/Shutterstock.com; p. 19 https://en.m.wikipedia.org/wiki/File:Gilbert_Stuart,_John_Adams,_c._1800-1815,_NGA_42933.jpg; p. 20 Everett Collection/Shutterstock.com; p. 21 Rosamar/Shutterstock.com; p. 22 https://commons.wikimedia.org/wiki/File:Jacques_Bertaux_-_Prise_du_palais_des_Tuileries_-_1793.jpg; p. 23 https://en.m.wikipedia.org/wiki/File:Surrender_of_Lord_Cornwallis.jpg; p. 25 stoker_1/Shutterstock.com; p. 26 Tamer A Soliman/Shutterstock.com; p. 27 https://en.m.wikipedia.org/wiki/File:BattleofLongisland.jpg; p. 28 Blueee77/Shutterstock.com; p. 29 John Gress Media Inc/Shutterstock.com.

Library of Congress Cataloging-in-Publication Data

Names: Schmidtt, Sarah, author.
Title: Exploring Washington's Farewell address / Sarah Schmidtt.
Description: Buffalo : Britannica Educational Publishing, an imprint of
  Rosen Publishing, 2025. | Series: Discover more: exploring primary
  sources | Includes index.
Identifiers: LCCN 2024033756 | ISBN 9781641903905 (library binding) | ISBN
  9781641903899 (paperback) | ISBN 9781641903912 (ebook)
Subjects: LCSH: Washington, George, 1732-1799. Farewell address. |
  Washington, George, 1732-1799--Influence. | United States--Politics and
  government.
Classification: LCC E312.952 .S365 2025 | DDC 973.4/1092--dc23/eng/20240819
LC record available at https://lccn.loc.gov/2024033756

Manufactured in the United States of America

Some of the images in this book illustrate individuals who are models. The depictions do not imply actual situations or events.

CPSIA Compliance Information: Batch #CWBRIT25. For further information contact Rosen Publishing at 1-800-237-9932.

Contents

Famous Last Words 4
Breaking Free 6
Organizing the Government 8
America's First President............ 10
An Advising Cabinet 12
Saying Goodbye.......................14
United in One Nation 16
A Warning Against Parties............18
Respecting Each Other 20
Neutrality.......................... 22
Faith in the Constitution 24
Danger of Debt 26
Washington's Legacy 28
Glossary 30
For More Information...................31
Index.................................32

Famous Last Words

George Washington, the first president of the United States, had been elected to office twice by 1792. After eight years as president, he had no interest in a third term. Before departing from office, he wanted to thank the citizens of the United States. He also wanted to inspire the new country to grow strong and remain an independent nation. He delivered this advice in a letter called Washington's Farewell Address. It was published in a Philadelphia newspaper on September 19, 1796.

Washington wrote in a diary for most of his life. Entries from the diaries help us to understand more about him and the time he was alive, so it is considered a primary source.

Washington worried if he died while still being president, Americans would view the presidency as a job to be held for life.

Washington's Farewell Address is a primary source. By studying it, we can learn more about the first U.S. president as well as what life was like back then. Primary sources are direct accounts of historical events or time periods, such as artifacts, documents, photographs, and any other source of information created during the time being studied. Secondary sources are also helpful in learning about the past, but they were created after the time being studied.

Consider This

Washington's diaries are a primary source, while a book written about Washington by someone who never knew him would be a secondary source. How might the diaries and other primary sources help someone to write about Washington?

Breaking Free

In the early 1600s, the king of Great Britain began establishing colonies in America. At first, the colonists had lots of freedom even though they were under British rule. They chose their own leaders and made their own laws.

In the 1750s and 1760s, the British and colonists fought the French and Indian War against the French. It was very costly. Britain taxed the colonies to help pay for the war. Colonists were mad about being taxed, especially because they had no representation in British government.

Washington was chosen as commander in chief of the Continental army because he was strong, had military experience, and could hopefully unite the colonies.

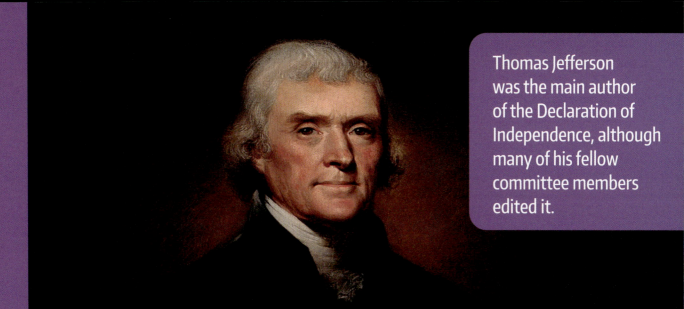

Thomas Jefferson was the main author of the Declaration of Independence, although many of his fellow committee members edited it.

In 1775, the colonists began fighting the American Revolution to win their freedom from Britain. George Washington led the colonial armed forces. On July 4, 1776, representatives of the thirteen colonies signed the Declaration of Independence. It states that "all men are created equal" and their rights include "life, liberty and the pursuit of happiness." With the Declaration's signing, the colonies were free from Great Britain.

Consider This
Is the Declaration of Independence a primary source? Why or why not?

Organizing the Government

The Battle of Yorktown, the final battle of the American Revolution, was an American victory led by General Washington in 1781. Two years later, the Treaty of Paris was signed, and the United States became an independent country. The Articles of Confederation served as the country's first constitution, or code of laws. Soon, however, the people realized there were problems with the document. In 1787, Washington served as president of the Constitutional Convention that met to design a new government.

The leaders at the Convention wrote the Constitution to establish a federal government. The Constitution defined how the national government would share power with the states. It organized the government into three equal branches—legislative, executive, and judicial. The legislative branch makes laws. The executive branch puts into use, or executes, the laws that the legislative branch makes. The judicial branch is a system of courts that interprets laws according to the Constitution to settle legal cases.

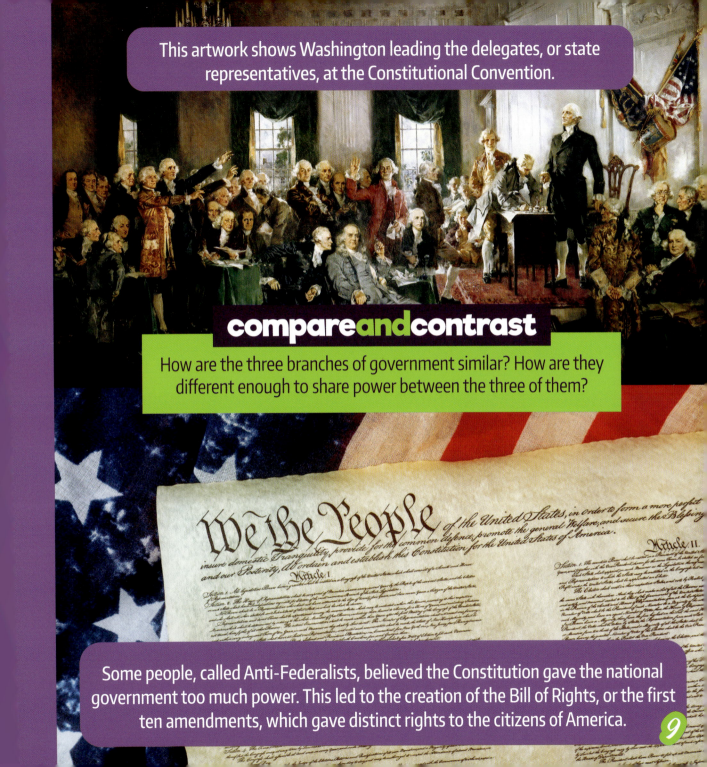

This artwork shows Washington leading the delegates, or state representatives, at the Constitutional Convention.

compare and contrast

How are the three branches of government similar? How are they different enough to share power between the three of them?

Some people, called Anti-Federalists, believed the Constitution gave the national government too much power. This led to the creation of the Bill of Rights, or the first ten amendments, which gave distinct rights to the citizens of America.

9

America's First President

By June of 1788, most of the states had ratified the Constitution. Congress set March 4, 1789, as the date for the new government to begin. A group of men called electors then chose Washington to be the country's first president. Washington took the oath of office in New York City on April 30, 1789. He was reelected in 1792. John Adams was his vice president.

George Washington was sworn in as president at Federal Hall in New York City. Hundreds of citizens gathered at the hall to watch Washington take his oath.

Washington presented the first presidential inaugural address to the nation. Every president since Washington, including 46th President Joe Biden (pictured with First Lady Jill Biden), has given an inaugural address.

Washington was elected unanimously, which means that everyone voted for him, both times. People from all the states respected Washington's leadership during the Revolution. They thought he could keep the states unified. Keeping this unity would be a major theme in Washington's Farewell Address.

In 1790, Washington approved a permanent location for the United States capital on the Potomac River. It would become known as Washington, D.C. As the new city was being planned and designed, the U.S. capital was changed from New York City to Philadelphia

Consider This

It does not say in the Constitution that a president must give an inaugural address, but Washington chose to do so. Why do you think he did this? Why has every president after him followed in his footsteps?

An Advising Cabinet

When he became president, Washington wanted a group of people around him to take on certain tasks and provide their own perspectives on issues. So, he set up a group of advisers to help him lead the country. The Constitution says the president is the head of the executive branch. Washington had to appoint officials who would answer to him. He formed a team called a cabinet. It had four members. The secretary of state was in charge of foreign affairs. The secretary of the Treasury dealt with all government money matters. The attorney general helped with all legal matters. There was also a secretary of war. The members of the cabinet were Washington's most trusted counselors.

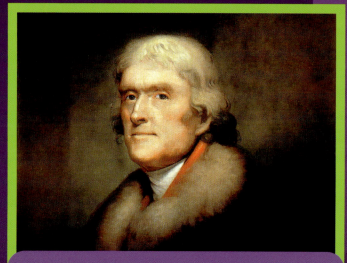

Thomas Jefferson was the United States's first secretary of state. He eventually became the third president of the United States.

Alexander Hamilton was the United States's first secretary of the Treasury. Hamilton's portrait is still on the U.S. ten-dollar bill today.

Washington liked to get different views. Both Thomas Jefferson and Alexander Hamilton were in his cabinet. Hamilton was a Federalist, or supporter of a strong central government. As a Democratic-Republican, Jefferson defended the power of the states. Washington was more favorable toward the Federalist ideals of government, but he remained **nonpartisan** and worked to sustain a balance between the two parties.

WORD WISE
NONPARTISAN MEANS A LACK OF OFFICIAL ASSOCIATION WITH ANY POLITICAL PARTY.

Saying Goodbye

Near the end of his second term as president, Washington was sixty-four years old and experiencing health problems. His eyesight and hearing were failing. Many wanted him to run for a third term. They felt he was the only man popular enough to keep the country together. Some people in the southern states were even threatening to start a separate country.

After his presidency, Washington retired to his home in Mount Vernon, Virginia. Many visitors traveled to see his home after he moved back there, and many visitors still come to see the home today!

Alexander Hamilton worked closely with Washington to help him write his farewell address. This means that Washington was not the only author of the article.

Washington knew it was time to step down, but he wanted to tell the country how important it was to stay unified. So, in his last year as president, he wrote his farewell address to the American people. He called on the United States to stay unified, resist the rise of political divides, and avoid the influence of foreign powers.

Consider This

Today, it is common for many public figures to have others help them write speeches and articles. Why might it be helpful for them to have another writer working with them?

United in One Nation

Above all else, Washington wanted to emphasize the preservation of the United States in his address. He thought that without unity the country could fall. He addressed his "Friends and Fellow Citizens," saying, "The unity of government which constitutes you one people is also now dear to you. It is justly so, for it is a main pillar in the edifice of your real independence; the support of your tranquility at home, your peace abroad; of your safety; of your prosperity in every shape; of that very liberty which you so highly prize." This means that the union of the states is the basis of many good things, such as independence, tranquility (or peace), and prosperity (or wealth and success).

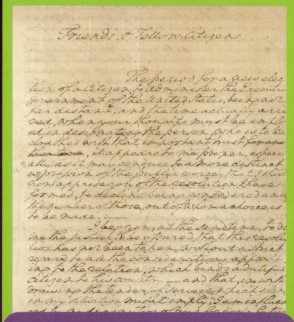

This is the first page of Washington's handwritten address.

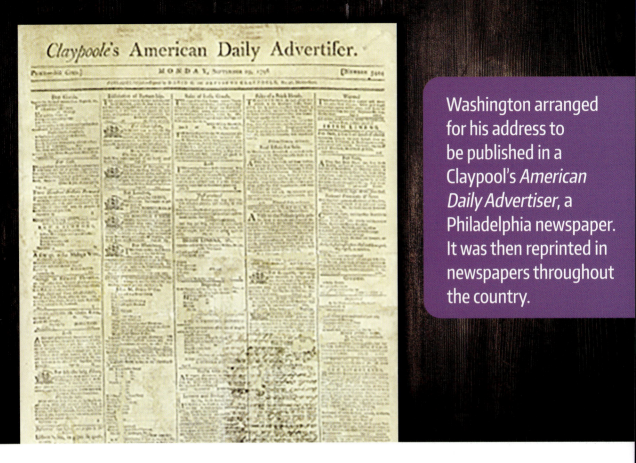

Washington arranged for his address to be published in a Claypool's *American Daily Advertiser*, a Philadelphia newspaper. It was then reprinted in newspapers throughout the country.

He also encouraged Americans to appreciate their country. "You should properly estimate the immense value of your national union to your collective and individual happiness." He encouraged Americans to "always exalt the just pride of **patriotism**."

WORD WISE
PATRIOTISM IS A LOVE AND PRIDEFULNESS FOR ONE'S OWN COUNTRY.

A Warning Against Parties

Washington feared that political groups promoting their own interests could lead to a destruction of the United States. He warned of "the baneful effect of the spirit of party," which referred to groups working for themselves rather than for the common good. He thought a political party was often "a small but artful and enterprising minority" that would "put in the place of the delegated will of the Nation, the will of [the] party."

Today's largest political parties are the Democratic Party (symbolized by a donkey) and the Republican Party (symbolized by an elephant).

Washington's vice president, John Adams, who eventually became the second U.S. president, was a member of the Federalist Party.

Washington argued that if one political party gained too much power it could unfairly dominate the party that was out of power. That party could rule unfairly. That is why he pushed to have parties restrained. As written in his address, "the common and continual mischiefs of the spirit of party are sufficient to make it the interest and duty of a wise people to discourage and restrain it."

Consider This

Why do you think Washington warned against political parties? How might they lead to divides in a country?

Respecting Each Other

George Washington was not known for being a great thinker or an extroverted person. The American people, however, loved his character. Washington was known to be honest, which is how the story of him chopping down a cherry tree developed. (The myth is that when his father confronted the young George Washington about chopping a tree, he replied, "I cannot tell a lie . . . I did cut it with my hatchet [small axe].")

The cherry tree myth has continued for more than two hundred years, but historians at both Washington's childhood home and Mount Vernon have said it's untrue.

Washington has been called the American Cincinnatus. Like Washington, Roman leader Cincinnatus led his people through hard times and retired afterward.

Washington believed that the country could succeed only through decent behaviors that show respect to fellow humans. Washington himself was always a man who emphasized duty, sacrifice, and honor. In his farewell address, he wrote, "Of all the dispositions and habits which lead to political prosperity, religion and **morality** are indispensable supports." He also stated that religion and morality are the "great pillars of human happiness" and the "firmest props of the duties of men and citizens."

WORD WISE
MORALITY IS A CONCERN FOR WHAT'S RIGHT AND WRONG, AS WELL AS WHAT'S GOOD AND BAD BEHAVIOR.

Neutrality

When war broke out in Europe between France and other countries in 1793, Washington decided the United States would remain neutral, or not help and support either side of the conflict. France had helped the colonies during the American Revolution. Because of that, the United States had promised to help France in any future conflicts, but Washington felt the United States was not prepared to enter another war so soon.

After the people of France overthrew their king, a war broke out between France and other countries. It has since been known as the French Revolutionary Wars.

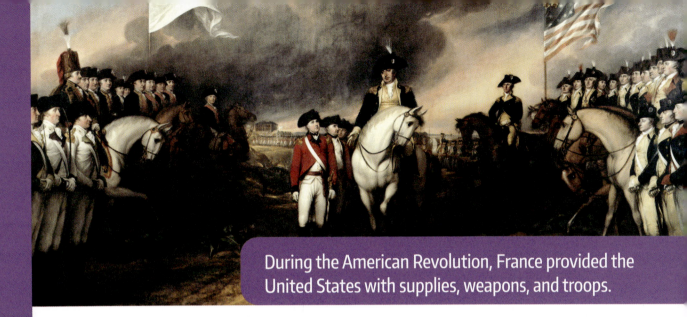

During the American Revolution, France provided the United States with supplies, weapons, and troops.

Washington was trying to keep the new country together. He thought that getting involved in a war might destroy the United States. In his farewell address, Washington highlighted his belief in neutrality. While he believed foreign "commercial relations" could be helpful, he urged the United States to "steer clear of permanent alliances" and have "as little political connection as possible." However, he wrote that temporary alliances could be made for "extraordinary emergencies."

Consider This

Many people believe the United States would've lost the American Revolution without France's help. Do you think Washington was correct for not helping France during their Revolution? Why or why not?

Faith in the Constitution

In his farewell address, Washington expressed that the Constitution would not steer the United States in the wrong direction. He supported the checks and balances in the Constitution. The checks and balances are the ways that each branch of the government limits the power of the others. He warned against letting "the powers of one department . . . encroach upon another," or letting one area of government take power away from another.

Washington reminded his fellow citizens that the Constitution could be amended, or changed. He believed this made the Constitution stronger, not weaker. As he wrote in his address, "The basis of our political system is the right of the people to make and to alter their constitutions of government. But the constitution which at any time exists, till changed by an explicit [detailed] and authentic [genuine] act of the whole people, is sacredly obligatory upon all."

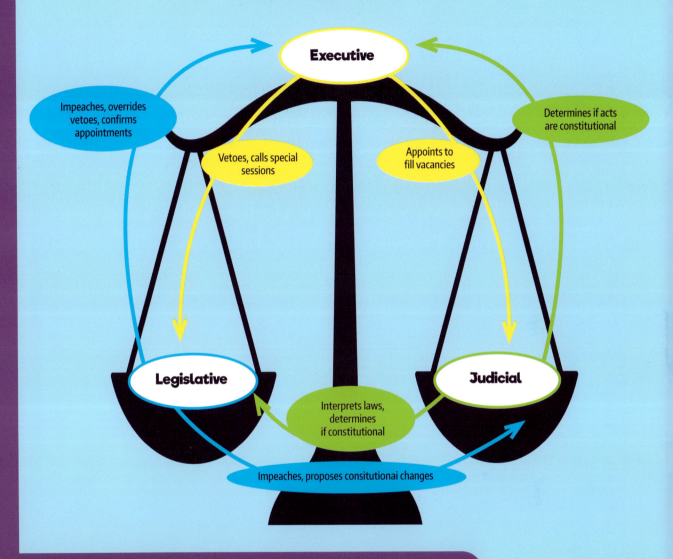

This illustration explains how the three branches of government limit each other through checks and balances.

Danger of Debt

At times, the national government spends more money than it makes, usually through the collection of taxes. To pay for everything, the government must borrow. The national debt is the total amount the United States has borrowed. Washington warned about taking on too much debt as a country. He thought if the country owed too much it would be weak. He wrote that debt should be used "as sparingly as possible."

As of 2024, the United States's national debt is over $30 trillion.

The United States borrowed over $2 million from France during the American Revolution. Some of the money went toward paying soldiers.

Washington knew that wars could be expensive. He advised that the country avoid "occasions of expense by cultivating [growing] peace." If debt could not be avoided, Washington said the government should do everything possible to pay off debt in times of peace. Still, if debts had to be paid, Washington told citizens that taxes are necessary. He understood that taxes were "inconvenient and unpleasant," but believed it was an American's duty to pay them.

Consider This
What would Washington think of the national debt today?

Washington's Legacy

Washington's Farewell Address remains an important and influential primary source in U.S. history. It shows the issues faced by a then-young United States, as well as how the country's first leader felt about the issues. The wisdom and advice in Washington's address continues to live on, as many other political leaders throughout history have turned to his words for guidance. Both President Andrew Jackson and President Abraham Lincoln talked about Washington's call for a strong union.

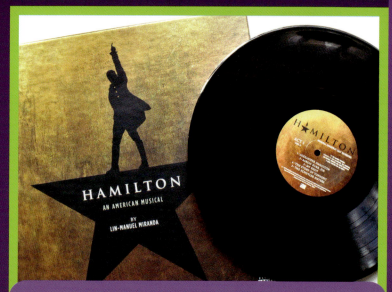

One of the lines in the song "One Last Time" features George Washington's character singing, "If I say goodbye, the nation learns to move on. It outlives me when I'm gone."

During President Barack Obama's farewell address on January 10, 2017, he frequently quoted Washington's address and warned the country about threats to democracy.

For years, American schoolchildren were taught to memorize the farewell address. The U.S. Senate continues to maintain a tradition of reading the address every year on Washington's birthday. The popular 2015 musical *Hamilton* also features a song about writing the address called "One Last Time," in which actual lines of the address are featured.

Consider This
Do you think the United States has followed the advice given by Washington? Why or why not?

Glossary

alliance An agreement between two or more countries.
artifact An object created by people that teaches something about the past or a particular culture.
baneful Causing serious damage.
collective Having to do with a group of people.
colonist A settler in a colony.
commercial Related to buying or selling goods.
confederation An organization that consists of a group of parties united in an alliance, or a group joined together for mutual benefit.
constitute To make up something.
Constitutional Convention A convention of delegates from all U.S. states (except Rhode Island) that met to write a new constitution.
document A written or printed piece of information that serves as an official record.
edifice A complex system of beliefs.
encroach To enter or force oneself on another's property or rights little by little.
exalt To praise highly.
extroverted A person who is outgoing and socially confident.
federal Relating to central government. Also, a form of government where states share power with a central government.
inaugural The beginning of an activity or time in office.
indispensable Absolutely necessary.
oath A formal promise to do something.
obligatory Not to be left out, forgotten, or ignored; required.
perspective Point of view.
preservation Keeping something from injury, loss, or decay.
ratify Sign or give formal consent to.
representation Standing or serving on behalf of another.
restrain To limit or control.
sacred Deserving respect or honor.
unity The quality or state of being combined as one single unit.

For More Information

Books

Huddleston, Emma. *George Washington*. Lake Elmo, MN: Focus Readers, 2023.

Messner, Kate. *The Next President*. San Francisco, CA: Chronicle Books, 2020.

Rajczak, Michael. *What Are Checks and Balances?* Buffalo, NY: Gareth Stevens Publishing, 2022.

Websites

Britannica Kids: Checks and Balances
kids.britannica.com/students/article/checks-and-balances/630952
Learn more about the government system Washington advocated for called checks and balances.

Homeschool Pop: George Washington for Kids
www.youtube.com/watch?v=2X9f2waOKU8
Watch this interesting video about George Washington's life and presidency.

Washington's Farewell Address
www.senate.gov/artandhistory/history/resources/pdf/Washingtons_Farewell_Address.pdf
Read Washington's full Farewell Address here.

Publisher's note to educators and parents: Our editors have carefully reviewed these websites to ensure that they are suitable for students. Many websites change frequently, however, and we cannot guarantee that a site's future contents will continue to meet our high standards of quality and educational value. Be advised that students should be closely supervised whenever they access the internet.

Index

A
Adams, John, 10, 19
American Revolution, 7, 8, 11, 22, 23, 27
Articles of Confederation, 8

B
Battle of Yorktown, 8
Biden, Joe, 11
Bill of Rights, 9

C
cabinet, 12, 13
checks and balances, 25
colonies, 6, 7
Congress, 10, 29
Constitution, 8, 9, 10, 12, 24
Constitutional Convention, 8, 9

D
Declaration of Independence, 7
debt, 26, 27
diary, 4, 5

F
French and Indian War, 6

G
Great Britain, 6, 7

H
Hamilton, 28, 29
Hamilton, Alexander, 13, 15

J
Jackson, Andrew, 28
Jefferson, Thomas, 7, 12, 13

L
Lincoln, Abraham, 28

O
Obama, Barack, 29

P
political parties, 18, 19

T
taxes, 6, 26
Treaty of Paris, 8